D1258522

Digging Up
DIRT
The Muckrakers

Sean Price

Chicago, Illinois

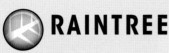
RAINTREE

TO ORDER:
☎ Phone Customer Service **888-454-2279**
💻 Visit **www.heinemannraintree.com** to browse our catalog and order online.

©2009 Raintree
a division of Pearson Education Limited
Chicago, Illinois

Editorial: Adam Miller
Design: Ryan Frieson, Kimberly R. Miracle, and Betsy Wernert
Photo Research: Tracy Cummins
Production: Victoria Fitzgerald

Originated by DOT Gradations Ltd
Printed and bound in the United States of America

ISBN-13: 978-1-4109-3117-7 (hc)
ISBN-10: 1-4109-3117-X (hc)
ISBN-13: 978-1-4109-3126-9 (pb)
ISBN-10: 1-4109-3126-9 (pb)

13 12 11 10 09
10 9 8 7 6 5 4 3 2

Library of Congress Cataloging-in-Publication Data
Price, Sean.
  Digging up dirt : the muckrakers / Sean Price.
    p. cm. -- (American history through primary sources)
  Includes bibliographical references and index.
  ISBN 978-1-4109-3117-7 (hc) --
  ISBN 978-1-4109-3126-9 (pb)
  1. Journalism--Social aspects--United States--History--20th century--Juvenile literature. 2. United States--Social conditions--20th century--Juvenile literature. 3. Journalists--United States--Biography--Juvenile literature. I. Title.
  PN4888.S6P75 2008
  302.23'097309042--dc22
                    2008011294

Acknowledgments
The author and publisher are grateful to the following for permission to reproduced copyright material: ©AP Image/Tracey Nearmy **p. 26**; ©Corbis **pp. 4, 5, 16-T, 21** (Bettmann), **11** (Frances Benjamin Johnston), **19-T**; ©Getty Images **pp. 28 (APA), 29**; ©The Granger Collection **pp. 7, 9, 20**; ©Library of Congress Prints and Photographs Division **pp. 6, 10, 12, 13, 14, 15, 16-B, 17, 18, 19-B, 22, 23-B, 23-T, 24, 25-B, 25-T, 26**.

Cover image of a group of breaker boys in Pittston, Pennsylvania, used with permission of ©Library of Congress Prints and Photographs Division.

The publishers would like to thank Nancy Harris for her assistance in the preparation of this book.

Contents

The First Muckrakers

Nellie Bly was scared. She was put in an **insane asylum**. In the 1800s, people with mental problems were put in places called asylums. Nellie did not have mental problems. But she pretended that she did.

Nellie was a reporter. Nellie worked for a newspaper. It was called the *New York World*. Nellie was working undercover. She wanted to see how mentally ill people were treated.

They were treated very badly. Many were beaten. They were also given little food. The little food they got was sometimes full of bugs. The asylum was supposed to help people. Instead, it was like a bad prison. Nellie spent ten days there. After that, she wrote stories about what happened. Her stories shocked people. They helped bring about changes.

This is Nellie Bly. She took big chances to get important stories.

Bly worked for the *New York World*. It ran her stories about the insane asylums. People read that asylums mistreated the sick people.

Nellie was one of the first **muckrakers**. They were a special type of writer. Muckrakers liked to dig for facts. They wrote stories about wrongdoing. Their stories often led to big changes.

5

muckraker   writer who reveals wrongdoing

How the Other Half Lives

Muckrakers were not just writers. Some used a camera, as well. Jacob Riis was a photographer. He took pictures in New York City. He showed how poor people lived. He put his photos in a book that he wrote. The book was called *How the Other Half Lives*.

Many of the poor that Riis showed were **immigrants**. They are people who moved to the United States from other countries. Poor immigrants lived in **tenements**. They are a kind of apartment building. Many tenements were rundown. They did not keep out the cold. They caught fire easily. Few had running water. Even so, immigrants were charged high prices. Greedy people made money off poor immigrants.

Jacob Riis was an immigrant from Denmark. He became successful. But he made people know how bad life was for poor immigrants in New York City.

immigrant   person who comes to the United States from another country

tenement   type of apartment building

Tenements could be terrible places to live.

Riis's book shocked people. New Yorkers made many changes that Riis called for. They made **laws** (rules) that said tenements must be built better. They also created schools and parks in poor areas. These changes made life better for many immigrants.

McClure the muckraker

Many **muckrakers** wrote for magazines. S.S. McClure owned some of those magazines. One of his most famous was *McClure's Magazine*. McClure wanted to identify big problems. He wanted to find out why bad things happened.

For instance, railroad companies were very powerful. McClure wanted to find out how they got their power. His writers found that many railroad companies broke **laws** (rules). They often cheated customers. People liked finding out these things. It helped them to understand their world. They bought magazines like *McClure's*.

Many magazines wrote articles to please rich people. Rich people had more money to buy magazines. But McClure tried to reach a wider group. He wanted all people to have good magazines to read.

Other magazines watched what McClure did. They saw that people talked about the articles in his magazines. Those magazines began to run muckraking articles. They wanted to have people talk about them, too. Muckraking became more widespread thanks to McClure.

HISTORY OF STANDARD OIL BY Ida M. Tarbell

MC.CLURE'S MAGAZINE

NOVEMBER

PUBLISHED MONTHLY BY THE S. S. McCLURE CO., 141-155 E. 25th ST., NEW YORK CITY

10 Norfolk St., Strand, London, W. C., Eng. Copyright, 1902, by The S. S. McClure Co. Entered at N.Y. Post-Office as Second-Class Matter

McClure's Magazine became famous for its muckraking articles. This issue ran muckraking stories about the oil industry.

The Cry of the Children

A lot of children worked in the early 1900s. These children came from poor families. Businesses liked to hire children. They could be paid less than adults.

John Spargo was a writer. He wrote a book called *The Bitter Cry of the Children*. Spargo showed how hard work hurt children. He showed that boys in Pennsylvania worked in **coal mines**. A mine is a hole in the ground where coal is found. Many worked as **breaker boys**. Breaker boys picked rocks out of coal. The air they worked in was full of coal dust. A disease called "black lung" was common. It came from breathing too much coal dust. Many died at a young age.

Children did hard work in places like coal mines. Child workers could be as young as six. But most were teenagers.

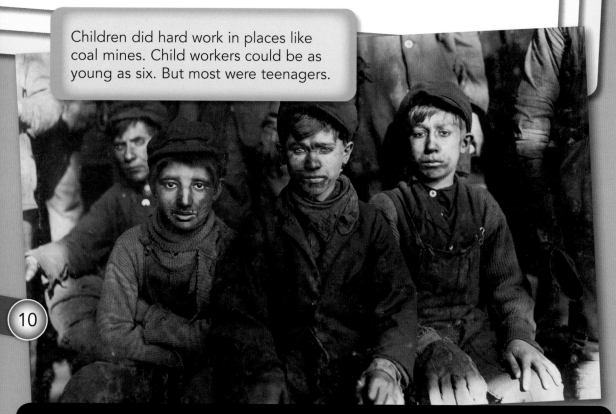

coal mine   place in the ground where coal is found
breaker boy   boy who picked rocks out of coal

Other businesses treated child workers badly. Some children worked at carpet factories. Carpet makers used **dyes**. Dyes are a type of paint for cloth. Many dyes are poisonous. Children were poisoned by these dyes. Some lost their lives. Others had life-long health problems.

Many young people worked as breaker boys. Their job was to separate coal from rocks. They spent hours seated on benches. This work was both hard and boring.

dye type of paint that colors cloth

The woman who toils

Most women did not work in the early 1900s. They stayed at home. They cleaned house and looked after kids. But poor women and girls did work.

These women led hard lives. Many worked at factories. Marie Van Vorst decided to see how they lived. She got a job at a pickle factory. Other women and girls worked at the factory. Their work was very hard. They had to stand for hours. People longed to sit down.

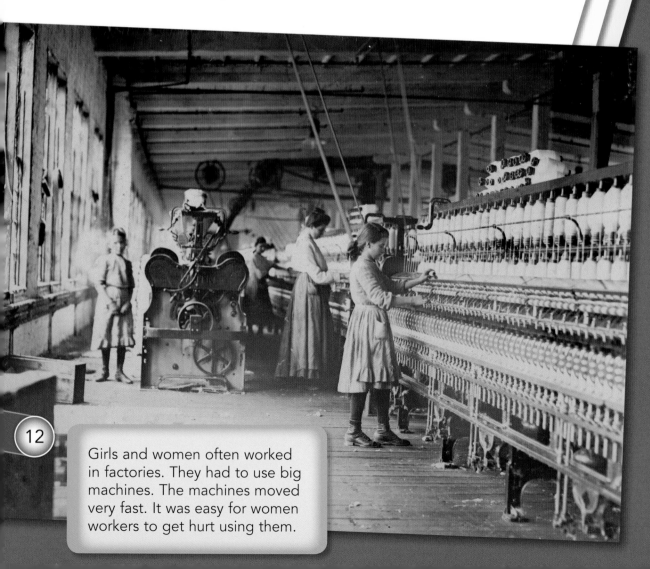

Girls and women often worked in factories. They had to use big machines. The machines moved very fast. It was easy for women workers to get hurt using them.

These women are shucking (opening) oysters. Each of them has a very sharp knife. They stick these into the shell to open them up. It's a very dangerous job!

Their jobs were also boring. People did the same thing all day. They stopped paying attention to what they were doing. This caused great danger. These workers had to use fast-moving machines. A careless worker might get hurt.

At one point, Van Vorst worked at a machine that put corks in bottles. If done wrong, the machine broke the bottles. That sent glass flying at workers. "Cuts is common," one worker told Van Vorst. "My hands is full of them."

Lewis Hine's camera

Lewis Hine was a photographer. He was against child labor. A group asked him to photograph kids at work. Hine went around the country and took pictures.

Many factories did not want Hine to take pictures. The owners knew that child labor was wrong. But they had children work for them anyway. Hine had to be clever about how he asked permission. He fooled owners. He told them he was taking pictures for other reasons.

Machines in textile mills put tiny bits of cloth in the air. These girls breathed in the cloth dust all day. It hurt their lungs and made it hard to breathe.

The men who hired children

Sarah N. Cleghorn was a writer. She wrote a well-known poem about child labor. It made fun of men who hired children.

The golf [course] lies so near the mill
That almost every day
The laboring children can look out
And see the men at play.

Lewis Hine took this picture in a bed factory. These boys are putting together bed springs. This was very dangerous because the springs were sharp!

Hine made many photos. Some of his best photos show work in **textile mills**. They were places where cloth and thread were made. Hine showed the dangerous work these children did. His photos became famous.

textile mill place where cloth and thread are made

Healthy Changes

Many **muckrakers** wrote magazine articles or books. But some wrote **novels**. Novels are made-up stories. Upton Sinclair was a muckraker who wrote a novel. It was called *The Jungle*. The events in *The Jungle* were based on real life.

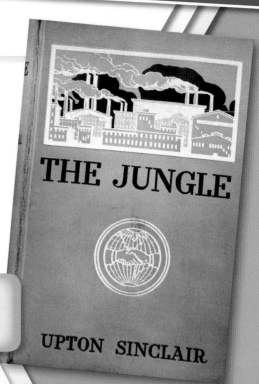

Sinclair's novel, *The Jungle*, came out in 1906.

Sinclair wrote it about the Chicago Stockyards. That is where cows and pigs were killed and turned into meat. Most Americans got their meat from these stockyards. Sinclair worked in the stockyards. He found out shocking things about how meat was made.

Sinclair wanted to show how hard life was for the workers. But readers were more shocked by the dirty conditions where meat was made!

novel book with a made-up story

These workers are cutting up pigs. It was a very dangerous job. Injuries were common.

Sinclair saw that rats and mice crawled all over the meat. Often dead rats were put into meat grinders. So was meat from cows with diseases. Rotten meat was also used. Sinclair wrote about a worker who fell into a giant mixer. He died. His body was mixed in with **lard**. Lard is animal fat used as grease for cooking. The lard was sold to people.

Many people refused to believe *The Jungle*. But others found that Sinclair's novel was based on truth.

lard   animal fat used as grease for cooking

Medicines that make you sick

Food was not the only thing that was unsafe. Many medicines were also very dangerous. In 1906, *Collier's* magazine showed the dangers of medicines. *Collier's* ran articles about **patent medicines**. These were medicines that could be bought without a prescription. A **prescription** is a note from a doctor.

Collier's showed that many patent medicines did not work. Others contained dangerous chemicals that actually hurt people.

Cleaning up food and medicine

Stories about rotten meat made people angry. So did stories about dangerous medicines. Americans called for new **laws** (rules). The new laws were passed in 1906. One was the Pure Food and Drug Act. The other was the Meat Inspection Act. Laws like these protect us still. They make sure we have safe food and medicines.

patent medicine   medicine that anyone can buy without help from a doctor
prescription   note from a doctor. It says a person should get medicine.

This ad is for a popular patent medicine for children. It was made from very dangerous and powerful drugs!

Companies made patent medicines. These companies made big promises. They said that their medicines could cure almost anything. But patent medicines cured nothing. Many contained dangerous drugs. People became hooked on these drugs. People could get very sick or even die from them. Some of these drugs were in cough syrups. Others were given to kids to help them sleep.

This ad is for a patent medicine that promised to cure headaches and other aches and pains.

Fighting the Powerful

Life was hard for black Americans in the early 1900s. Many white people did not like them. They thought blacks were not as good as whites. Many whites wanted black people to obey them. If blacks disagreed, they might be killed.

Many blacks were **lynched**. That meant groups of white people killed them. These groups were called **lynch mobs**. Often lynch mobs hung blacks. They killed blacks in other ways, too.

Ida B. Wells-Barnett spoke out strongly against lynching. Her articles caused a lot of anger in the South. That is where the most lynchings took place.

Angry people joined lynch mobs. Many claimed that lynch mobs only attacked criminals. Wells-Barnett showed that this was not true.

Ida B. Wells-Barnett was a black writer. Three friends of hers were lynched. She started writing about lynch mobs. Many blacks who were lynched were said to be criminals. Wells-Barnett showed that they had done nothing wrong. Whites had simply been angry at them.

Whites became angry at Wells-Barnett. They smashed her newspaper press. She had to leave town. But she still wrote about lynching. Her work raised awareness about lynching. But it was many years before **laws** or rules stopped it.

Shame of the cities

Big cities were controlled by **bosses**. They were powerful men. Many bosses were **public officials**. A public official is voted for or chosen by the people. They are chosen to help lead a city or town.

Bosses kept power in many ways. One way was to help the poor. A boss might find a poor man a job. He might give the man's family a turkey at Thanksgiving. In return, poor people voted for the boss.

This picture shows two bosses with a tiger in front of Tammany Hall. The bosses controlled New York City. People called this group the "Tammany Tiger."

boss powerful man who was often elected to his job

Tammany Hall is where the bosses worked.

Lincoln Steffens wrote about Tammany bosses. He also wrote about bosses in other cities. He showed how they stole money from the public.

Lincoln Steffens wrote for *McClure's Magazine*. He showed how bosses got rich. They stole money from their cities. Bosses also hurt poor people in secret. Poor people lived in rundown buildings. Bosses took money from the building owners. The bosses did nothing to make the buildings better or safer. The owners charged poor people high prices.

Steffen's articles were made into a book. It was called *The Shame of the Cities*. This book opened the eyes of many people who had supported bosses.

23

Standard Oil was very powerful. This cartoon shows how many people viewed the company.

The octopus of oil

Ida Tarbell also worked for *McClure's Magazine*. She looked into how businesses cheated people. The oil industry had not been around for long. But it was very powerful. At that time, one company controlled oil in the United States. The company was Standard Oil.

Standard Oil was owned by John D. Rockefeller. Tarbell looked into how Rockefeller took control of the oil business. She showed that he forced people to do what he wanted. Rockefeller broke the **law** (rules). He had even bombed other companies.

Rockefeller's control of oil was unfair. He could raise the price of oil very high. People had to buy it at that price. They didn't have any choice. This made Rockefeller very rich.

John D. Rockefeller made Standard Oil a huge company. He also became one of the world's richest men.

Ida B. Tarbell showed that Rockefeller did many unfair things. He broke laws and cheated to make Standard Oil so powerful.

Tarbell's stories about Rockefeller changed people's view of Standard Oil. Within a few years, the company was broken up. It was broken into several smaller companies. That gave people more choices for buying oil. It helped keep prices down.

Silencing the muckrakers

Powerful people did not like **muckrakers**. They attacked muckraking magazines.

In 1910, railroads shut down *Hampton's Magazine*. *Hampton's* ran muckraking articles. Magazines like *Hampton's* made money by selling ads. Companies buy ads in magazines to sell their goods. The railroads pressured companies that bought those ads. They told those companies that they would lose railroad business. *Hampton's* could no longer sell ads. The magazine lost money and had to close.

The making of "muckraker"

The name "muckraker" came from President Theodore Roosevelt. He was the country's leader from 1901 to 1909. Roosevelt became angry at writers who exposed problems. He called them muckrakers as an insult. But muckraking writers liked the name.

Eric Schlosser and other writers like him are modern-day muckrakers.

Efforts like this hurt muckrakers. But muckraking never died out. In fact, muckraking is still with us today. There are many examples. In 2001, Eric Schlosser wrote a book called *Fast Food Nation*. It showed how unhealthy fast food can be. Since then, fast food stores have tried to offer more healthy food.

Baseball's "Black Sox"

Muckrakers are not always popular. Sometimes their stories make people mad. In 1920, Hugh Fullerton ran a story that angered people in Chicago.

Fullerton's story was about the Chicago White Sox. They are a Major League baseball team. Fullerton said the Chicago White Sox cheated. They cheated in the 1919 **World Series**. The World Series is the championship of baseball.

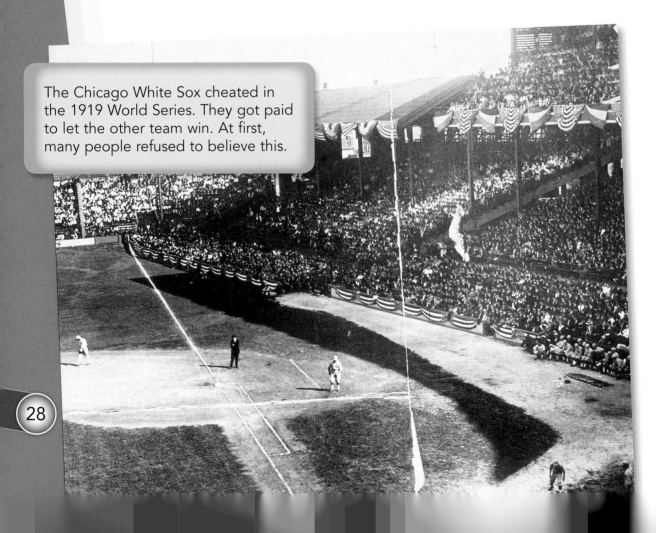

The Chicago White Sox cheated in the 1919 World Series. They got paid to let the other team win. At first, many people refused to believe this.

Eight White Sox players were kicked out of baseball. People started calling them the "Black Sox."

Fullerton said the White Sox lost on purpose. They did this to help **gamblers**. Gamblers bet money. The gamblers knew the White Sox would lose. So they bet money on who would win the World Series. Others did not know that the White Sox would lose. So the gamblers made a lot of money.

People did not believe Fullerton's story. But soon there was more proof that he was right. People became angry with the White Sox players. Eight players had cheated. All eight had to leave baseball. Baseball teams soon made it harder for players to cheat.

29

Glossary

boss powerful person who was often elected to his job

breaker boy boy who picks rocks out of coal

coal mine place in the ground where coal is found

dye type of paint that colors cloth

gambler someone who bets money that something will happen

immigrant person who comes to the U.S. from another country

insane asylum place where mentally ill people were put

lard animal fat used as grease for cooking

law rule

lynch to kill

lynch mob group of people that kills someone

muckraker writer who reveals wrongdoing

novel book with a made-up story

patent medicine medicine that anyone can buy without help from a doctor

prescription note from a doctor. It says a person should get medicine.

public official person who is elected or chosen by the people for a job.

tenement type of apartment building

textile mill place where cloth and thread are made

World Series championship of baseball

Want to Know More?

Books to read

Bausum, Ann. *Muckrakers: How Ida Tarbell, Upton Sinclair, and Lincoln Steffens Helped Expose Scandal, Inspire Reform, and Invent Investigative Journalism.* Washington: National Geographic, 2007.

Gallagher, Aileen. *The Muckrakers: American Journalism During the Age of Reform.* New York: Rosen Central, 2006.

Hakim, Joy. A History of US: Book 8: An Age of Extremes, 1880–1917. New York: Oxford University Press, 2002.

Websites

http://www.pbs.org/wnet/jimcrow/stories_people_wells.html
Find out more about Ida B.Wells-Barnett's crusade against lynching.

http://www.pbs.org/wgbh/amex/world/sfeature/memoir.html
Read more about the exciting life of Nellie Bly.

http://www.historyplace.com/unitedstates/childlabor/index.html
Go here to see more of Lewis Hine's powerful photos.

Places to visit

Newseum
555 Pennsylvania Ave., N.W. • Washington, DC 20001 • Call (888) 639-7386
http://www.newseum.org

Read ***Dirty Thirties: Documenting the Dust Bowl*** to learn about the dust storms that swept across the midwestern United States during the 1930s.

Index